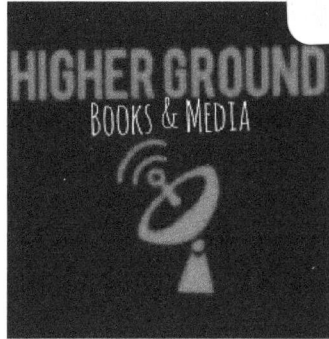

Higher Ground Books & Media

Higher Ground Books & Media
Springfield, Ohio.
http://www.highergroundbooksandmedia.com

Printed in the United States of America 2019

Talking it Over with Him

Learning through Daily Prayer

By Rebecca Benston

FOREWORD

Several years ago, God began to speak to me. I wasn't sure what was happening, but I knew that I had to make some big changes in my life or it wasn't going to be worth living. I was in an unhappy marriage; one that failed to offer me the peace and security of a loving husband. Instead, I felt insecure and at times even threatened by his lack of understanding and compassion for the things that I was going through. All the while, I was certain that his failure to love me was somehow my fault. I didn't know how wrong I was.

Over the last several years, some things came to light. Since then, I've been keeping prayer journals each day and as I've gone back to look at where I've been and where He's been with me, I have been amazed by the connections that I didn't see at the time I was praying the prayers. It has recently been placed on my heart to try and connect the dots between the prayers that He has given me and the lessons I learned as a result of them. I feel that His intention was for me to share these prayers with you.

So this book, the first of many to come, is my testimony about one of the most difficult periods in my life as a born-again Christian. I hope that what I share here will not turn you away, but instead will help you see that no matter what you think you may have done you are never so far away from God that He will not lift you up out of despair. I hope that this book blesses you and that you can begin to heal through witnessing the healing work that Christ has done in my heart and my life.

God bless!

Each chapter includes a section for taking notes. I encourage you to use these pages during your prayer time to make a note of the important messages and insights that you receive as you study God's word.

(All taken from NIV unless otherwise noted)

Notes from God: 2/16/11
Beginning to Listen

For several years now, God has spoken to me through a series of verses that He gives me during prayer time or even during church services. I've tried to sort out the messages that He has given and put them into some cohesive context.

Ecclesiastes 3:12-I know that there is nothing better for people than to be happy and to do good while they live.

These words from God came to me as I began to seriously study His word and try to understand what He might be saying to me. The very first thing He wanted me to know and hide deep within my heart was that His desire for me is and always has been that I would be happy and do good while I live. My life is not to be wasted on pettiness, bitterness, anger and fear. For many years, I set myself up to be surrounded by people and things that would bring me just the opposite of what His will was for me. And it worked. For a long time, I knew nothing but those things and the idea of peace was a foreign concept to me. I wasn't even sure it existed.

John 4:26- Then Jesus declared, "I, the one speaking to you—I am He."

Yes, sometimes He has to be this direct with us. When we have failed to listen and we continue to run headlong down the wrong path, sometimes He just has to step in front of us, stick out his leg and let us trip over our own stupidity. Standing over me on more than one occasion, He has spoken those words to me, "I, the one speaking to you—I am He!!!!" Now quit messing around, we've got work to do.

Ezekiel 3:8- But I will make you as unyielding and hardened as they are.

And the question always comes, once I've gotten up and allowed Him to brush the dust off of me and set me in the right direction. "What about the people who try to make me feel stupid for following You? How do I handle them? Am I right to follow You? Or have I just lost my mind?" The first year or so that I was really learning in to hear His voice, I was sure that I couldn't be what I needed to be. After all, I wasn't good enough to be a Christian. How could He possibly use me for anything worthwhile after the life I had led? All of these questions and His answer was always the same, "Do not be afraid of them or terrified by them, though they are a rebellious people." (Ezekiel 3:9)

2 Chronicles 2:16- and we will cut all the logs from Lebanon that you need and will float them as rafts by sea down to Joppa. You can then take them up to Jerusalem."

As Ezra writes in the book of 2 Chronicles, the task of taking the logs to Jerusalem was not easy. The meaning of all of this is to impress upon us that as believers, we must not be afraid to look at our past and to understand that simply not doing the things we once did is not enough if we wish to be free from sin. We must understand and embrace the difficulties that will come as a natural consequence of living our lives for God. The struggles may be difficult, but building a temple is hard work. Tearing down what has been destroyed and rebuilding from the ground up is even harder. But the rewards are eternal.

Ezra 4:6 - At the beginning of the reign of Xerxes, they lodged an accusation against the people of Judah and Jerusalem.

There will be great opposition, but you must not let that stop you from building the temple. Discouragement is the key weapon of the devil and he will use it at any cost. We are encouraged not to be fooled by the tricks and schemes of the evil one and to persevere.

Matthew 8:16- When evening came, many who were demon-possessed were brought to him, and he drove out the spirits with a word and healed all the sick.

Even when the devil has us in his clutches, Jesus has no problem healing us if we come to Him for rest and peace. He will restore those who have been touched by evil. And once we have turned back to him, there is nothing we can't do.

Psalm 32:11- Rejoice in the LORD and be glad, you righteous; sing, all you who are upright in heart!

When you have gotten this far, don't forget to rejoice in all that He has done for you. God wants us to acknowledge His goodness and to love Him back.

Some days I would get many verses from Him and He would tell me things that simply didn't make sense. On this particular day, I had two separate sets of verses. There were the ones from the morning which I've listed above and the ones from the evening, which I will now try to explain.

2 Timothy 3:12- In fact, everyone who wants to live a godly life in Christ Jesus will be persecuted,

Yes. I'm starting to see this. One of the first things God needed to show me was that I didn't need to be afraid to tell people I was a Christian. In fact, I should expect that no one would be too happy about it and that I would experience ridicule and persecution. As a matter of fact, it was right around this time that I had been struggling with the repercussions of letting people in my workplace know that I was a Christian.

Earlier that year, I had sent out an e-mail inviting people to join me at a fundraising event for a Christian outreach that actually functioned within our organization. I had used a Bible verse as a footer for my e-mail for at least a year and a half up to that point in time. When I sent out this invitation, my supervisor approached me and said that I needed to remove the verse. I asked her why and she said that it had offended someone. I thought about it for a moment and responded to her by saying that I was offended that she would ask me to remove it.

To make a long, painful story short, I ended up taking the matter before my union and was threatened with termination until I took the verse off of my e-mail template. Following this incident, my supervisor began to pick at me for every little thing and I racked up an amazing seven reprimands during that year. For those who don't know much about me, I have never really been in trouble. I am chronically compliant and have always had a healthy fear of authority. I was one of those kids in high school who never forgot homework, never had detention, never skipped school, etc. The idea that I would have ever found myself in trouble in a work setting was ludicrous. The only reason that I had this difficulty was because I had attempted to stand up for my faith. I later resigned due to the ridiculous pressures placed on me by that supervisor.

1 Corinthians 3:8- The one who plants and the one who waters have one purpose, and they will each be rewarded according to their own labor.

Learning our purpose is extremely important if we want to do something with our new-found faith. If we understand the Bible and the sermons we hear, but we fail to put that understanding into practice because we cannot connect it to the purpose He has created in us, then it does absolutely no good to have that knowledge.

Yes, there is one who is meant to plant the seed and one who is meant to nurture that seed and help it grow and mature. If you are not the planter, then you are either the nurturer or the one who is still awaiting a planting. Make sure you've removed the rocks and weeds from the soil of your heart so that when His word falls on you, it will be able to grow into something wonderful and powerful and worthy of the One who created you.

Hebrews 1:8- But to the Son He says, "Your throne, O God, will last for ever and ever; a scepter of justice will be the scepter of your kingdom.

Do not turn away from Christianity in order to escape persecution. His throne will live forever. He has already won this fight. He calls on your faith in Him as you go through the trials that are set forth by this world. He desires our devotion and it is that devotion that will enable us to emerge from any trial or tragedy victorious.

Proverbs 21:16- Whoever strays from the path of prudence comes to rest in the company of the dead.

In most cases, when we fail to continue on in our journey following Christ, we find ourselves keeping company with those who are dead in spirit. Prudence means care, caution, and good judgment. When we stop taking care to be deliberate in our pursuit of Jesus, we lose focus on why it is important to live a life that rises above the pleasures of this world. And so, we must not allow ourselves to become complacent. We must keep moving forward.

For me, I have a tendency to run my mouth when I feel I am being attacked or insulted. It gets me into trouble every time. And as I am preparing for a custody hearing at the time of this writing, these words hit me like a ton of bricks. I know that He is guiding me and telling me that I just need to be very careful with the words I choose to say. I need to be respectful to the judge and I need to answer all of my attorney's questions as succinctly as I possibly can. This won't be easy as I've felt like the court hasn't been listening or paying attention and when I finally get an opportunity to speak, I know that I will feel compelled to just blurt out everything that is on my mind. But I must be strong. I must listen for God's prompting before speaking and carefully consider my words. As long as I do this and am truthful in my responses, everything should be okay.

Notes

_____

_____

_____

_____

_____

_____

_____

_____

_____

_____

_____

_____

_____

_____

_____

_____

_____

_____

_____

_____

_____

_____

_____

_____

_____

_____

_____

_____

_____

_____

_____

_____

_____

Notes from God: 2/17/11
Learning to hear

Mark 4:16- Others, like seed sown on rocky places, hear the word and at once receive it with joy.

The Parable of the Sower has always been intriguing to me. I've often wondered which of these terrains represent my current state of heart. Sometimes, I am like the rocky ground where the seed is happily received, but isn't able to properly receive it. How do I take my heart from being so "rocky" to being a place where the seed can take root and thrive? The best way is through reading and studying God's word and asking questions like this.

Ecclesiastes 4:16- There was no end to all the people who were before them. But those who came later were not pleased with the successor. This too is meaningless, a chasing after the wind.

When I investigated the meaning of this verse, I found that it was referring to the ease with which those in power may find themselves in the position of having to beg. Thus, humility is essential if we are to have any success as God's children. Once we get to a place where we have the power to hurt or heal, we must always choose to heal or at the very least, do no harm. In my experience, too many women who find themselves in a position of power take the opportunity to step on other women in order to keep their own positions secure.

In my own case, when I was a supervisor, I was so scared of losing my position that I wasn't very understanding of the issues that the women working for me faced. And in turn, I gave them a hard time when I should have gone out of my way to support them. Thankfully, I later had the opportunity to apologize to one of them and let her know that I valued her and that I should never have been so hard on her.

I have been fortunate enough to work with more than a couple of ladies throughout my career who have been wonderful and I will never forget how they helped me overcome the obstacles that had been set in my path. Most recently, the women I work with during my day job continue to impress me with their confidence and their lack of cattiness. They seem to understand all too well that our situations can turn in an instant and the most important thing we can do is to be resilient and to build that same resilience in one another.

John 1:8-He was not that light, but was sent to bear witness of that light.

And this verse ties right into that idea that we must be willing to pave the way for others to lead. If we find ourselves in the position of having the power to make decisions and to effect change, we must look at the reasons why God would put us in those positions. It is never for the purposes of boosting our own egos or making us feel worthwhile. Sometimes, we must put aside our need to be important and understand that we are not the light, but that we are to be witnesses to the light that is in Christ. We must help others to bring the Christ out in everything they do and to do that; He must be the focus of everything we do.

Ephesians 2:13-But now in Christ Jesus you who once were far off have been brought near by the blood of Christ.

A reminder that no matter how far away we feel we are from Christ, we are never too far away to grab onto His hand and allow Him to pick us up. Even in a humbled state that we brought on ourselves, He will always show mercy because He knows that we are not perfect.

Galatians 5:7-You ran well, who hindered you from obeying the truth?

And He asks the question, even though He intends to show mercy. This conviction that He brings upon us causes us to feel uncomfortable in our sin, but it also shows us that He wants to understand what it is that can pull us away from Him. He wants to understand His creation and to help us be more like Him.

The problem we have most often is in feeling that once we have messed up, He won't want anything to do with us. The longer I walk with Him, the more I see that I'm going to spend the majority of my time messing up and only a small portion of it walking in the manner that He wishes me to walk. I'm a hot mess and He knows that I can't do any of this right without His help. He wants me to see it, too.

Esther 1:6-There were white and blue linen curtains fastened with cords of fine linen and purple on silver rods and marble pillars and the couches were of gold and silver on a mosaic pavement of alabaster turquoise and white and black marble.

As Esther probably felt out of place in such surroundings, I've often felt out of place as I've dwelt in the blessings of my Father. I've felt as though I was masquerading as something I was not and that when people found out that I was really not a good person, they would destroy me. I never accepted or acknowledged the protection that God provides in a way that convinced me fully that I was justified in walking with my head held high. Like it or not, I am a child of the King. Whether it makes sense or not, His royal blood flows through my veins and I have the Spirit of the Lord living in my heart. I may not know how to fully manifest it in all of my actions yet, but He's there and He is waiting for me to claim my place in His royal army.

Notes

_____

_____

_____

_____

_____

_____

_____

_____

_____

_____

_____

_____

_____

_____

_____

_____

Notes from God: 2/18/11
Something Big Will Happen

Obadiah 2:6-Behold I will make you small among nations; you shall be greatly despised.

Again, the message about the reversal of self-importance. This was broken off of me long before I started receiving these messages, but I feel that He was trying to prepare me for an attack of pride as I began to learn more about Him and His plan for me.

As a Christian, it can be too easy to start feeling superior to those who have not yet embraced their relationship with Him. This is a huge problem in the church. When we allow Him to wash us clean and cover our sins, we do not somehow become better than everyone else. We have just found out the secret to having more peace in our hearts about being just like everyone else; broken.

Yes, we are supposed to set ourselves apart from sin, but there is no way for us not to be human and not to have been born with a sin nature that will always try to take us over when we are making strides toward walking in the right direction with Him.

Esther 3:6- But he disdained to lay hands on Mordecai alone, for they had told him of the people of Mordecai. Instead, Haman sought to destroy all the Jews who were throughout the whole kingdom of Ahasuerus—the people of Mordecai.

When people are drunk with power, as Haman was, they tend to do a lot of damage. They hurt others and often they don't think past the initial action to the long-term repercussions of what they have done. And the more opportunities they have to abuse others, the less they care that they are doing it. Even if the abuse is turned inward and the only one they are technically hurting is their own self, there comes a point where the individual can become numb to the impact he or she is having on others. In Haman's case, he never seemed to become aware of just how awful he was being and God dealt with him in a manner that was consistent with the pain he had caused. Sadly, too many people never come to a place of repentance and their lives fail to have the peace and joy that comes from following hard after God.

John 4:10- Jesus answered and said to her, "If you knew the gift of God, and who it is who says to you, 'Give Me a drink,' you would have asked Him, and He would have given you living water."

How many times has Jesus been trying to speak to me when I've failed to recognize Him or just plain ignored what He was saying? More times than I can count…and probably more times than I would have even known I needed to count. If I had known it was Jesus, would I have responded differently? There have been times in my life when I'm not sure I would have even understood what it means to encounter Him…I had little understanding of who He was and of the sacrifice that He made to save my soul. Even now, as I long for a face-to-face meeting with Him, I still am not 100% sure that I would know Him even if He was right in front of me. Would He tell me as He did the woman at the well? Satan would have me believe that He wouldn't. That He would keep me guessing for as long as possible and the maybe, just maybe, He really doesn't care about me the way He says that He does.

2 Chronicles 2:16-And we will cut wood from Lebanon as much as you need; we will bring it to you in rafts by sea to Joppa.

This journey will not be easy. But it has purpose and the more faithful you are in walking the path, the greater your reward in Him will be.

Psalm 46:7-The Lord of hosts is with us. The God of Jacob is our refuge.

In all things and at all times, we need to remember that God is with us. Even when we feel as though we are far from Him, He is always within our reach. He allows us the time to make our mistakes and to lean on Him and accept His grace and love. Always, He is our strong tower and our shelter from the storm.

Numbers 4:4-This is the service of the sons of Kohath in the tabernacle of meeting; relating to the most holy things.

Being in relationship with the Lord is serious. It requires discipline and reverence for His holiness. Yes, He is our Father, but He is also to be Lord of our lives. We must allow Him to lead us and to write the story of our lives on our hearts. He is in control and He must be at the center of all things.

Luke 2:13-And suddenly, there was with the angel a multitude of the heavenly host praising God and saying...

In order to make sense of this verse, I had to step forward one and find that in 2:14, it says, ""Glory to God in the highest, and on earth peace, goodwill toward men!" An exclamation of devotion to the Lord God and an expression of joy at His love toward mankind. Just before this declaration, the angel had told the shepherds in the field that there would be a baby wrapped in swaddling clothes, born in a manger and that He would be the light of the world. The delivery of this message to the people was of great importance and it was meant to give them hope. In the same way, those who believe in Jesus are to go out and let the world know that He is Lord and that He will one day be coming back for His people. Just as the angel announced that He would be born that night, we are to announce that He is alive and coming back soon.

Malachi 2:16- "For the LORD God of Israel says that He hates divorce, for it covers one's garment with violence," says the LORD of hosts. "Therefore take heed to your spirit that you do not deal treacherously."

Interestingly enough, I was healing from the pain of divorce when this verse appeared in my daily prayer. It came up on more than one occasion and so, I decided that I would approach my ex-husband about fixing things. He wasn't willing and so, I had to press on. But this message, like any message in God's word, wasn't meant to shame me. God already knew that I couldn't reverse the divorce. He already knew that my ex-husband wasn't going to deal with me fairly. I believe that my willingness to ask his forgiveness and to offer to help fix the marriage was a big step toward my understanding of how we are to view our relationships with others. Although I could not repair the marriage, I did manage to allow God to repair my own brokenness and to help me understand the role I played in the failure of that union. The sad fact is that we can't always go back and receive the same level of forgiveness that we are offering to those we've abandoned or hurt, even if we didn't intend to inflict pain. If they aren't walking the same path or a path that leads to the same destination, they will not see our offer of forgiveness as anything of value. We can only be obedient to God and accept that His will may not have been for reconciliation in that particular case.

Notes

_____

_____

_____

_____

_____

_____

_____

_____

_____

_____

_____

_____

_____

_____

_____

_____

Notes from God: 2/19/11
"What now, Lord?"

2 Timothy 2:13- If we are faithless, He remains faithful; He cannot deny Himself.

And so, He lives in us. When we begin to accept Jesus as our personal Savior, He comes to live in us…or rather, His Holy Spirit does. It's a concept that many people can't get their minds around. But we are told that when Jesus died and was resurrected and then ascended to heaven once again, He told us that His Spirit would return to dwell with us. At this point in my prayer life, something became clear to me; we are so changed when we allow Jesus into our hearts that we cannot act the way we used to act. We have evicted the old self and taken on the Spirit of Christ. We no longer allow the Spirit of our flesh to rule our lives. And something happens that makes all of that sin so difficult for us to maintain. We may still do some things that we shouldn't do, but our reaction to what we are doing is different. The amount of satisfaction that comes from doing the wrong thing diminishes and we long for something better.

Jude 1:4- For certain men have crept in unnoticed, who long ago were marked out for this condemnation, ungodly men, who turn the grace of our God into lewdness and deny the only Lord God and our Lord Jesus Christ.

Beware of the men that creep in! Amen to that! One of the strongholds that I've fought with nearly all of my life had to do with my quest to find a man who would love me the way I wanted to be loved. And so, in my brokenness, I was vulnerable to all sorts of attacks. Mostly emotional and psychological, but a few were actually physical. I tend to have the ability to attract the most broken of men and to be disappointed by them time and again.

In this verse, the men they were referring to were in the church. Those who were attempting to make others believe in something that wasn't necessarily the right thing to believe in. They teach their own version of Christianity and their own interpretation of grace and its implications. These men were false teachers who hid behind God's word and who understood it on the surface, but had no real depth in it. It is basically the same issue, but in a different context. The impact is the same. A man who endeavors to love but has no love in his heart can only teach a shallow love to those who are attempting to learn from him. As a follower, we must be vigilant to find depth in the teaching and not just logic and information.

Hebrews 6:20-...where the forerunner has entered for us, even Jesus, having become High Priest forever according to the order of Melchizedek.

Assurances that He has paved the way for us to follow Him and that we need not be afraid to walk that path.

Daniel 1:14- So he consented with them in this matter, and tested them ten days.

As Daniel and his men held to their beliefs and refused to indulge in delicacies brought in for them by the king's men, they came out of it looking better and stronger than those who had no conviction about partaking. Often, those who are in sin believe that the "fun" they are indulging in is better for them that depriving themselves, but in the end when you look at them in comparison to a believer who is serious about following God, you see that they lack the joyful countenance of a heart that is at peace in the Lord.

Colossians 2:16- So let no one judge you in food or in drink, or regarding a festival or a new moon or Sabbaths...

Oddly, this verse speaks to not allowing others to dictate what you put into your body. The law stated that we were not to partake of certain foods and that we were to do things in accordance with the rituals of the day, but Jesus came to free us from that bondage. While He does not tell us to do whatever we want whenever we want, He does bring the message that ritualistic behavior will not guarantee a spot in heaven.   If we rely solely on trying to stay within the prescribed lines of behavior that men want us to follow, we will often miss the point of what it means to love as Christ loves.

Hebrews 2:11- For both He who sanctifies and those who are being sanctified are all of one, for which reason He is not ashamed to call them brethren…

Yes! When we allow Him to be the Lord of our lives, He shows us that we are worthy of His love. Our sanctification comes through our acceptance of His love in our lives and the reflection of that love to those around us.

Notes

_____

_____

_____

_____

_____

_____

_____

_____

_____

_____

_____

_____

_____

_____

Notes from God: 2/20/11
A Clear Sign

Jeremiah 2:18- And now why take the road to Egypt, to drink the waters of Sihor? Or why take the road to Assyria, to drink the waters of the River?

In these early days of learning, I often referred back to a concordance or commentary to try and make sense of what I was reading. I see now that He was trying to help me gain familiarity with what was in the Bible and He was shedding just enough light on His word to keep me from feeling like I was too dumb to "get it." This verse was listed as meaning that the question referred to leaving a great reward in order to go back in search of a broken existence. When we are living in sin, with no real understanding of the bondage we are in, we can be easily tempted to go back to what is familiar; finding comfort only in the fact that it is something we already know and that it doesn't require any learning or growth to maintain. The road to reward with Christ is not an easy one and it certainly doesn't seem to be a logical use of such limited time here on earth. Everything here points to living life to the fullest and getting the most satisfaction possible out of every little thing we do. To deny ourselves for a greater reward later is not a concept that most people readily embrace.

1 Samuel 3:11-Then the LORD said to Samuel: "Behold, I will do something in Israel at which both ears of everyone who hears it will tingle."

God is going to get the attention of those who fail to acknowledge them. Plain and simple, it will happen.

Zechariah 3:10- In that day,' says the LORD of hosts, 'Everyone will invite his neighbor under his vine and under his fig tree.'"

And He will bring peace and tranquility to those who have acknowledged Him.

2 Chronicles 6:18- "But will God indeed dwell with men on the earth? Behold, heaven and the heaven of heavens cannot contain You. How much less this temple which I have built!"

God was even willing to come and walk among us in order to have fellowship with us. This is how much He desires to have relationship with His children.

James 4:16-But now you boast in your arrogance. All such boasting is evil.

But going forward without including God in the plan is not going to work.

Deuteronomy 4:10-especially concerning the day you stood before the LORD your God in Horeb, when the LORD said to me, 'Gather the people to Me, and I will let them hear My words, that they may learn to fear Me all the days they live on the earth, and that they may teach their children.'

And not having a clear understanding of His word can be even more dangerous. Those whose interpretations are formed solely to justify actions that they refuse to give up are not serving God, they are sidestepping Him. When we acknowledge Him in all our ways, it means we obey Him in all things. It means that we seek to understand the true meaning and not just our spin on what was said. Yes, our upbringing and our backgrounds have a great deal to do with the way we approach God's word, but the truth of His word never changes and our ability to understand it is a direction reflection of our acceptance that His truth is the only truth that matters.

2 Timothy 1:15-This you know, that all those in Asia have turned away from me, among whom are Phygellus and Hermogenes.

And so, after we are tested, we are left with the truth of who we are. What remains once we have shed the flesh nature is something that God can work with.

Hebrews 11-13 (Entire chapters)

Daniel 2:32-This image's head was of fine gold, its chest and arms of silver, its belly and thighs of bronze,

I learned later, in one of the many Beth Moore Bible studies that I went through, that the symbolism here had to do with the power of each of these kingdoms. I believe this was in her study on Daniel. I found this to be one of the most interesting Bible studies I'd ever been in and I would highly recommend this to anyone who is seeking answers about end-time prophecy.

Notes

_____

_____

_____

_____

_____

_____

_____

_____

_____

_____

_____

_____

_____

_____

_____

_____

_____

_____

_____

_____

_____

_____

_____

_____

_____

_____

_____

_____

_____

_____

_____

_____

_____

_____

Notes from God: 2/21/11
Do Not Be Afraid

Ezekiel 2:6- And you, son of man, do not be afraid of them nor be afraid of their words, though briers and thorns are with you and you dwell among scorpions; do not be afraid of their words or dismayed by their looks, though they are a rebellious house.

Sometimes, you may be the only one in your circle of friends who "gets it" and those whom you love and whom you have hoped to protect or help will not take you seriously. They may always view you through the lens of who you once were and never give you credit for having made any progress toward having a true understanding of things. And so, they won't allow you to guide them out of their pit and toward the freedom that you have found. But, you cannot be afraid to keep walking. Either they will figure out that something has changed in you or they will hold to their belief that you have lost your mind. Remember, you don't answer to "them," you answer to Him.

1 Corinthians 4:16-Therefore I urge you, imitate me.

This is definitely easier said than done. Of course we want to be as much like Him as we possibly can once we have figured out that it is He who has given us everything we have. But the truth is, we will never be perfect. We can only hope to be as perfect as a human being can be and we achieve that perfection, ironically, once we stop being so preoccupied with what it means to be perfect.

Joshua 2:14- So the men answered her, "Our lives for yours, if none of you tell this business of ours. And it shall be, when the LORD has given us the land, that we will deal kindly and truly with you."

The reward for having faith that God will connect us to the right people and the right things once we surrender all to Him, is in the reality that our faith in Him is recognized by others who have faith in Him. And we draw strength from one another.

John 1:11- He came to His own, and His own did not receive Him.

As I indicated earlier, when we make progress, there will always be those who don't understand it, are intimidated by it, are afraid that we will think less of them, or otherwise decide that our move ahead is a threat to them. Often, we just need to move on and allow them to catch up when God moves them.

Ruth 4:18- Now this is the genealogy of Perez: Perez begot Hezron...

I have never fully understood why I got these verses. But I do know that having an understanding of the genealogy of Christ helps us to see that there was and is a grand design.

Colossians 1:26- the mystery which has been hidden from ages and from generations, but now has been revealed to His saints.

This seems to be how He does it. He reveals a little at a time as we are ready to receive that revelation.

Jude 2:13- Mercy, peace, and love be multiplied to you.

There is great comfort in knowing that this is what He wishes for us. And as we grow stronger in the knowledge of the Word, He entrusts more to us and allows us to grow even more.

Notes

_____

_____

_____

_____

_____

_____

_____

_____

_____

_____

_____

_____

_____

_____

_____

_____

_____

_____

Notes from God: 2/22/11
What Would Jesus Do?

Luke 2:13- And suddenly there was with the angel a multitude of the heavenly host praising God and saying:

I often get open-ended verses like this one. And I believe that it is because God is trying to break this need to know all of the answers off of me. Of course, if I read a few more verses, the answers are clear. But this is what He clearly speaks…that there was an angel praising God and saying…well…something. Perhaps the point is not what the angel was saying, but the fact that he is saying it. I have had a tendency to hold some things in from time to time and in doing so, I fail to publicly do enough of what the angel was clearly doing here…praising God.

Hosea 4:13- They offer sacrifices on the mountaintops,
And burn incense on the hills,
Under oaks, poplars, and terebinths,
Because their shade is good.
Therefore your daughters commit harlotry,
And your brides commit adultery.

While He is guiding me to speak His word freely, His word also warns me not to misuse His name. This means that I don't curse others in His name, I don't take oaths which go against His word, and I don't do anything that contradicts His word while claiming to be serving Him through what I'm saying or doing.

1 Corinthians 1:16- Yes, I also baptized the household of Stephanas. Besides, I do not know whether I baptized any other.

It really doesn't matter what great things others have done. It is what Christ has done that matters. We must be steadfast in maintaining our reverence for the One who has done the redeeming. While there may be many good people who do good things, there is only one Christ and He is to be honored and praised through the work that we do in His name. It's not about us.

2 Samuel 2:22- So Abner said again to Asahel, "Turn aside from following me. Why should I strike you to the ground? How then could I face your brother Joab?"

In studying this verse, I found that Abner wanted to avoid a blood feud. There had been much drama and he was all done with it. But, in the surrounding verses, we see that Asahel would not turn aside from him and so, Abner had no choice but to kill him. Sometimes, confrontation can be avoided. Sometimes we have to do the difficult thing even when what we want most is to walk away from conflict. Our enemies may see our unwillingness to fight as a sign of weakness, but we must understand that there is great strength in not inciting conflict. There is no shame in not wanting to perpetuate the fight, but there is also no shame in striking back when necessary. Trust in God to show you the right time to fight and the right time to walk away.

1 Timothy 3:8- Likewise deacons must be reverent, not double-tongued, not given to much wine, not greedy for money,

And we must follow the guidelines that God has set forth in His word if we are to accurately represent Him. We cannot make our decisions based on our own assessment of what is good and acceptable by our own standards. Our standards are almost always a great deal more relaxed than His standards for us. That is why we have so many self-righteous Christians who feel that they can dictate what is right and wrong while they are consistently missing the point of His entire message through Christ.

Galatians 4:12- Brethren, I urge you to become like me, for I became like you. You have not injured me at all.

And to become more like Christ, we cannot come to a place in our walk when we believe that we no longer have to try and understand our brothers and sisters. When we become too "holy" to reach out to those who haven't yet become acquainted with our God, we have become so far away from God's will for our lives that we are no longer qualified to testify. Never be too proud of yourself to tell others where He has been with you and what His grace has brought you through. He gives each of us a unique set of experiences and He asks us to walk it out and to reach for Him when the road becomes too treacherous. And once He has helped us through, we are to go forth and testify to His wonderful and undying love for us. It's as simple as that. He created us with a purpose and in His plans for us, He has set forth challenges as well as blessings so that we may exercise our faith and so that our love for Him will grow as we go through each season.

Notes

_____

_____

_____

_____

_____

_____

_____

_____

_____

_____

_____

_____

_____

_____

_____

_____

_____

_____

About the Author

Rebecca Benston is from Springfield, OH. She is the author of The Rona Shively Stories mystery series which currently includes ten books. Benston has also written several inspirational books including Rise Up to Wise Up, a companion guide to her women's empowerment group workshops. Benston's work was previously published through Stonegarden Books. In 2014, Stonegarden closed its doors and she was faced with an important decision; continue writing and seek another publisher or publish her own work and help other authors tell their stories. She decided on the latter and Books from Higher Ground (BHG) was born. In 2017, the name was changed to Higher Ground Books & Media. To date, Benston has signed 35 additional authors, one of which is her own daughter, Mya Benston. She continues to reach out to authors, young and old, encouraging them to tell the stories that God has placed on their hearts. Every soul has a testimony and it is Benston's mission to get those stories to their intended audiences.

Higher Ground Books & Media does not charge a fee to publish. It is not a vanity press. It is an independent publishing company that pays royalties to the author based on a standard author contract. If you have a story to tell, please contact Rebecca at highergroundbooksandmedia@gmail.com or visit the website at http://www.highergroundbooksandmedia.com for more information on submission guidelines.

You can check out what HGBM has to offer at http://www.highergroundbooksandmedia.com

Other titles from Books from Higher Ground:

Wise Up to Rise Up by Rebecca Benston

A Path to Shalom by Steen Burke

365 Days of Family Fun by Charlotte Hopkins

From a Hole in My Life to a Life Made Whole by Janet Kay Teresa

Overcomer by Forrest Henslee

Miracles: I Love Them by Forest Godin

32 Days with Christ's Passion by Mark Etter

The Magic Egg by Linda Phillipson

The Tin Can Gang by Chuck David

Whobert the Owl by Mya C. Benston

Add these titles to your collection today!

http://www.highergroundbooksandmedia.com

9 781949 798319